NAME:

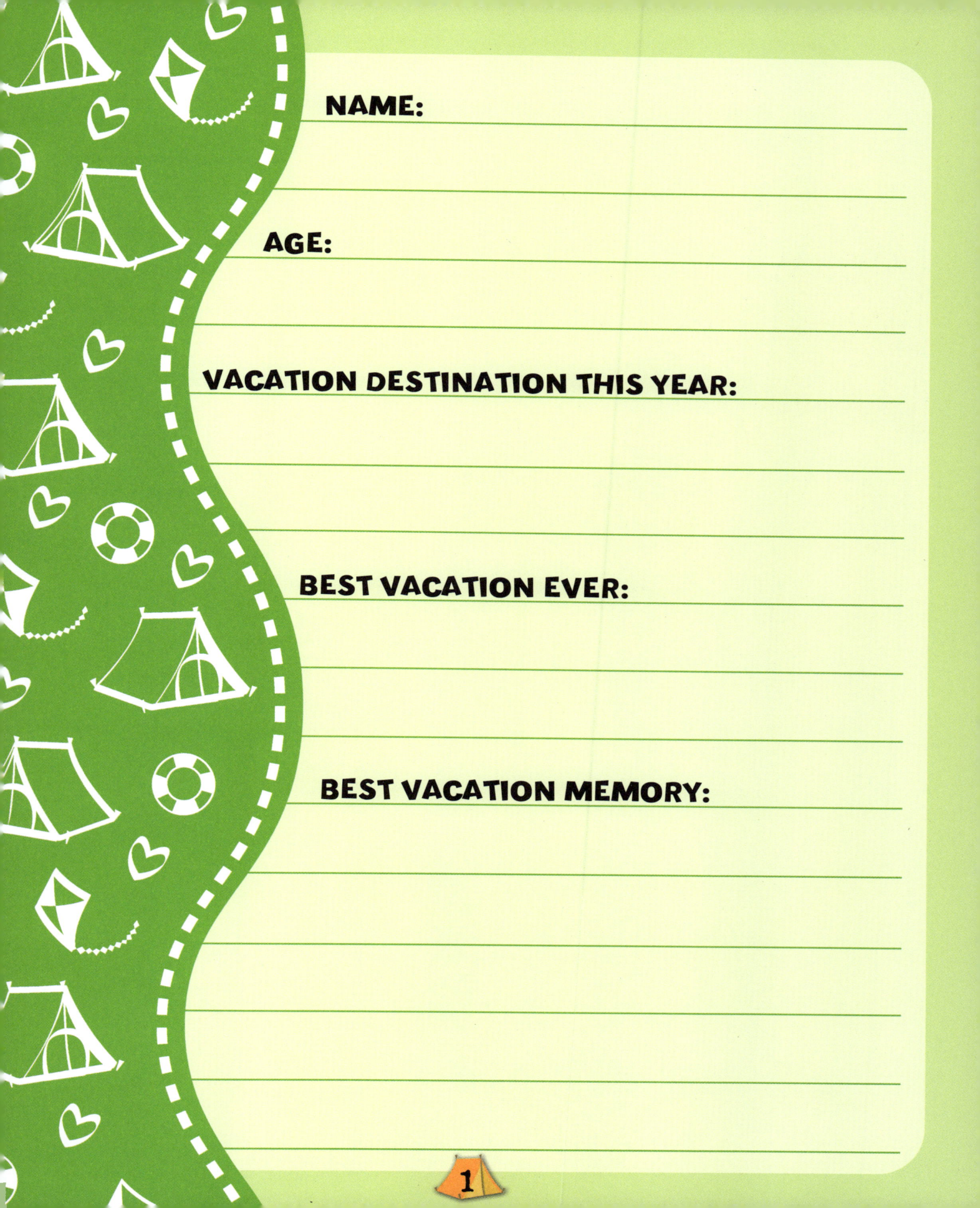

AGE:

VACATION DESTINATION THIS YEAR:

BEST VACATION EVER:

BEST VACATION MEMORY:

Practice packing for your vacation. What essentials will you need? Draw them in the suitcase. Have you forgotten anything?

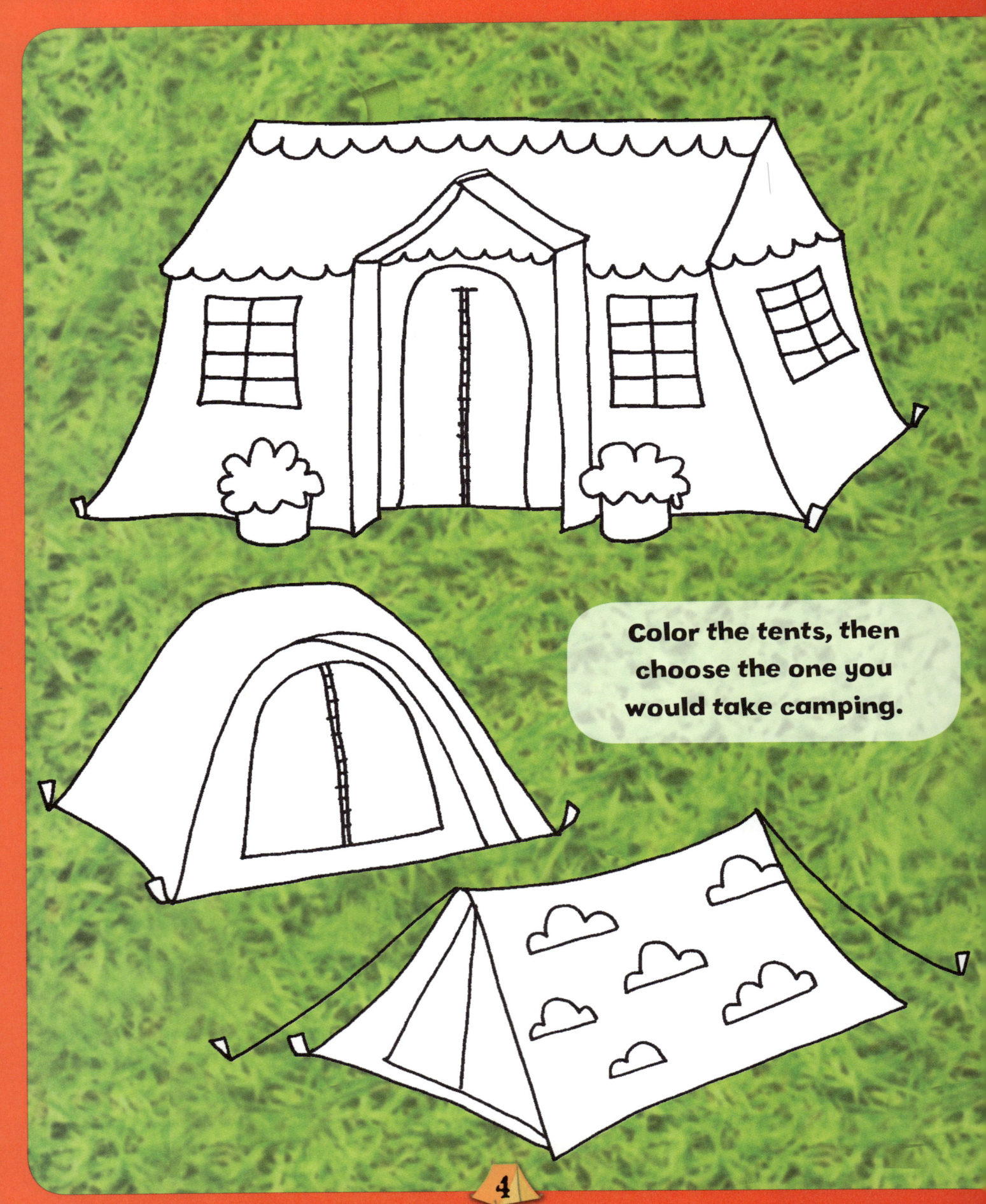

Believe it or not, this game is actually a sport in some countries. The best way to play is with lots of competitors in a wide, open space.

You will need: one rain boot or galosh per competitor, open space, bucket to mark throwing point, an adult, and a named marker for each competitor.

How to play:

1 Each competitor, in turn, stands in line with the bucket holding the boot. They face away from the open area.

2 The adult checks that no one has strayed into the open area - a boot on the head will hurt! When clear, they call "Rain boot away!" or "Galosh go!"

3 The competitor now throws the boot over their shoulder.

4 The competitor who has thrown the boot the furthest is the champion.

8

There are some really scrumptious treats you can make when camping.
*** Adult supervision is required at all stages.**

Toasted marshmallows

You will need: adult supervision, campfire or barbecue, long stick, and marshmallows.

1. Securely thread a marshmallow (or two) onto the stick, near the tip. The stick has to be long enough that you are a good distance from the fire.

2. Hold the marshmallow just above the flames so that it heats up (and becomes gooey) and toasts (rather than burns) to a pale honey color.

3. Remove the stick from above the fire. Let the stick and marshmallow cool before removing the marshmallow. Yummy!

Chocolate bananas

You will need: adult supervision, campfire or barbecue, one banana (skin on) per serving, block of chocolate, and kitchen foil.

1. Ask an adult to slice each banana from end to end through the skin, but only partway into the banana.

2. Push three or four squares of chocolate into the opening. Wrap each banana in foil, making sure that the chocolate-stuffed side is at the top.

3. When the fire or barbecue is dying, ask an adult to lay the bananas on the coals. Leave to bake for about 15 minutes.

4. When cooked, remove the bananas from the coal with tongs or oven gloves and remove the foil. Spoon the chocolate banana onto a plate. Delicious!

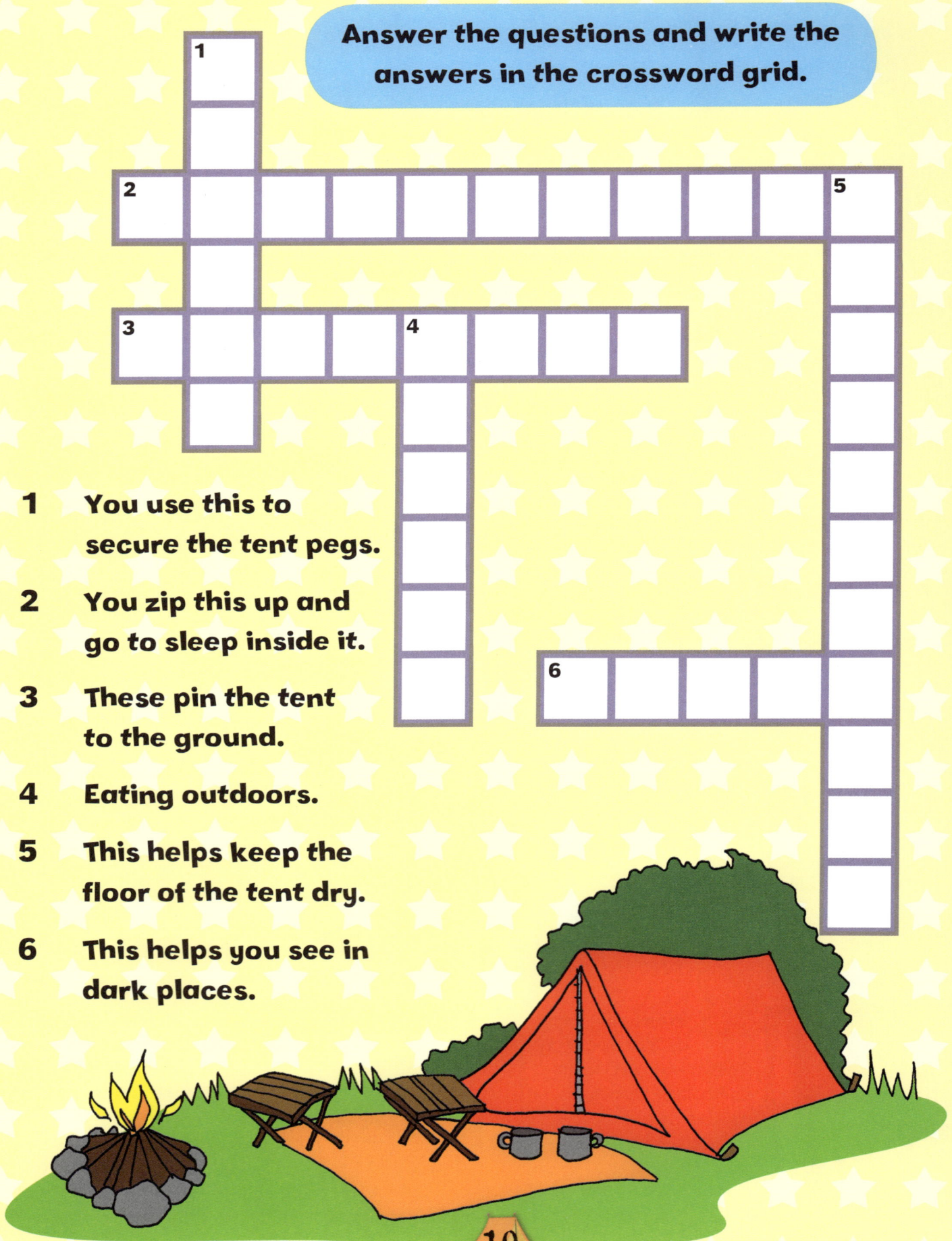

All the fun of fishing without getting wet.

You will need: one or more players, colored paper, scissors, paperclips, and one each of the following per player – stick or plant cane, one yard of string, one small horseshoe magnet.

1 Trace the templates (opposite) onto colored paper and cut out. Make as many as you like. Number the fish 1 to 6 with a felt-tip marker. (This is for scoring later on.)

2 Attach one paperclip onto each paper sea creature.

3 Tie a length of string to the tip of each stick or cane. Secure the string with a piece of tape.

4 Tie a magnet to the free end of each piece of string. Secure with a piece of tape.

How to play: Throw the paperclip sea creatures into the 'water'. The players stand an agreed distance from the 'water' and dangle their rods to pick up the paperclip fish. Keep fishing until there are no fish left in the 'water'. Add up the scores. The player with the largest score wins.

- flowery rain boots
- 2 striped tents
- soccer ball
- 4 barbecues
- dog running away with sausages

Find the words below in the wordsearch grid. Watch out – some words are backwards!

```
N O C A B D N A S G G E
S W O L L A M H S R A M
K V U A B S P Z A Y I O
N H S F O W Y C L I P S
L R E G R U B M A H W T
L T Y Z C I D G D T K W
O E R L H O T D O G F A
A N A N A B D E K A B P
G O J T M V I Q N N Q L
U T B C A J G L P O G O
B A K E D P O T A T O W
B H V M Q P E A X A S R
```

Marshmallows   Baked potato   Salad   Hamburger

Hot dog   Eggs and bacon   Baked banana

Postcards
Press out the two postcards and write your message on the back.

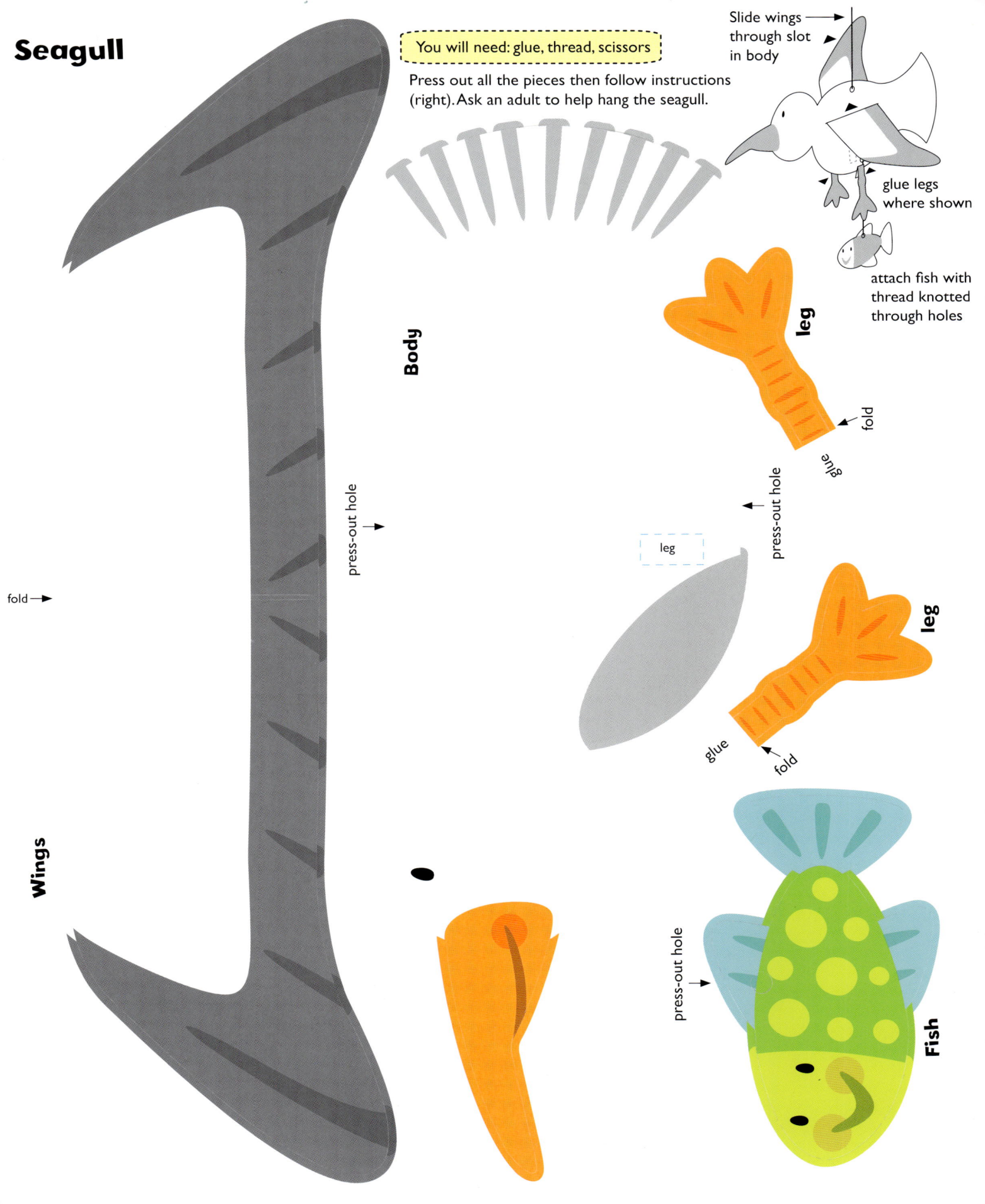

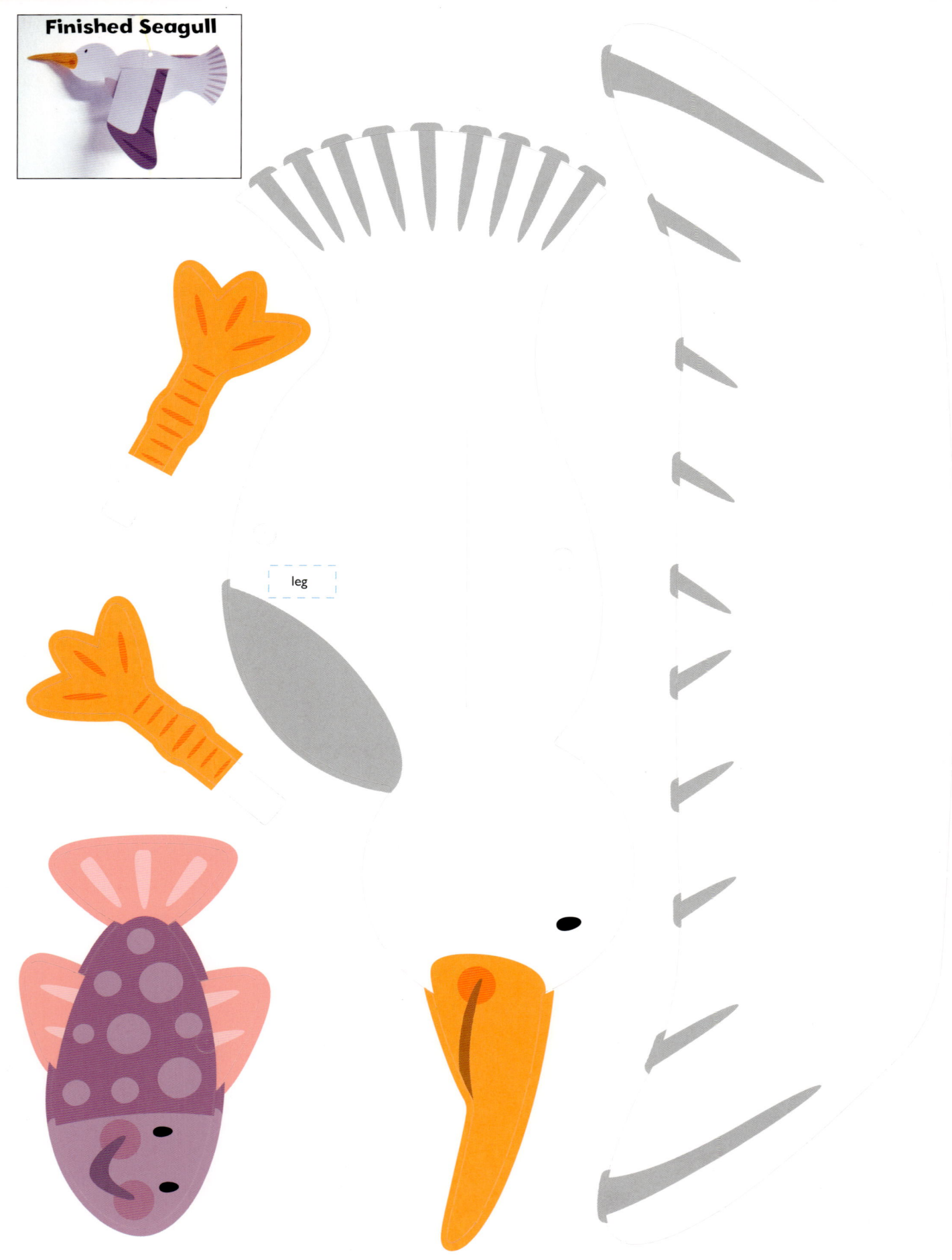

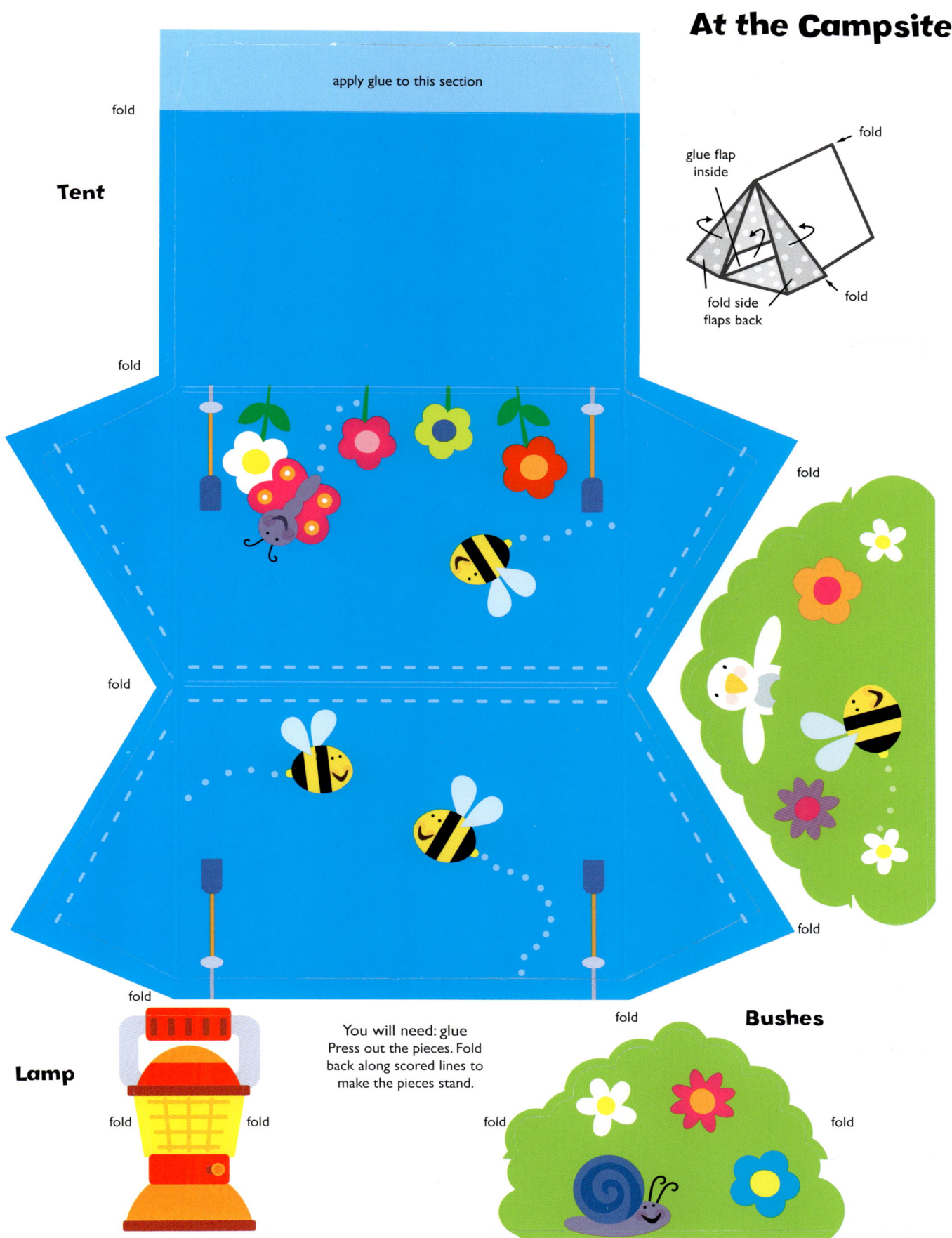

These kids have spotted some animal shadows outside their tent. Can you recognize what they are?

a _____
b _____
c _____
d _____
e _____

It's good to recycle your garbage, so why not turn it into art?

Collect some bits and pieces that you might normally throw away – magazines, bottle tops, paper plates, candy wrappers, and popsicle sticks, for example. These can be turned into art.

Wash things like bags, popsicle sticks, and bottle tops to make sure they are clean.

Use a clean sheet of thick paper and some craft glue to assemble and arrange a collage.

You could also ask if you can use some dried pasta and fabric remnants.

It's amazing what you can create with almost nothing!

Figure out what is at each grid reference on the map.

b4 _____   d5 _____

f1 _____ h2 _____

g5 _____ i4 _____

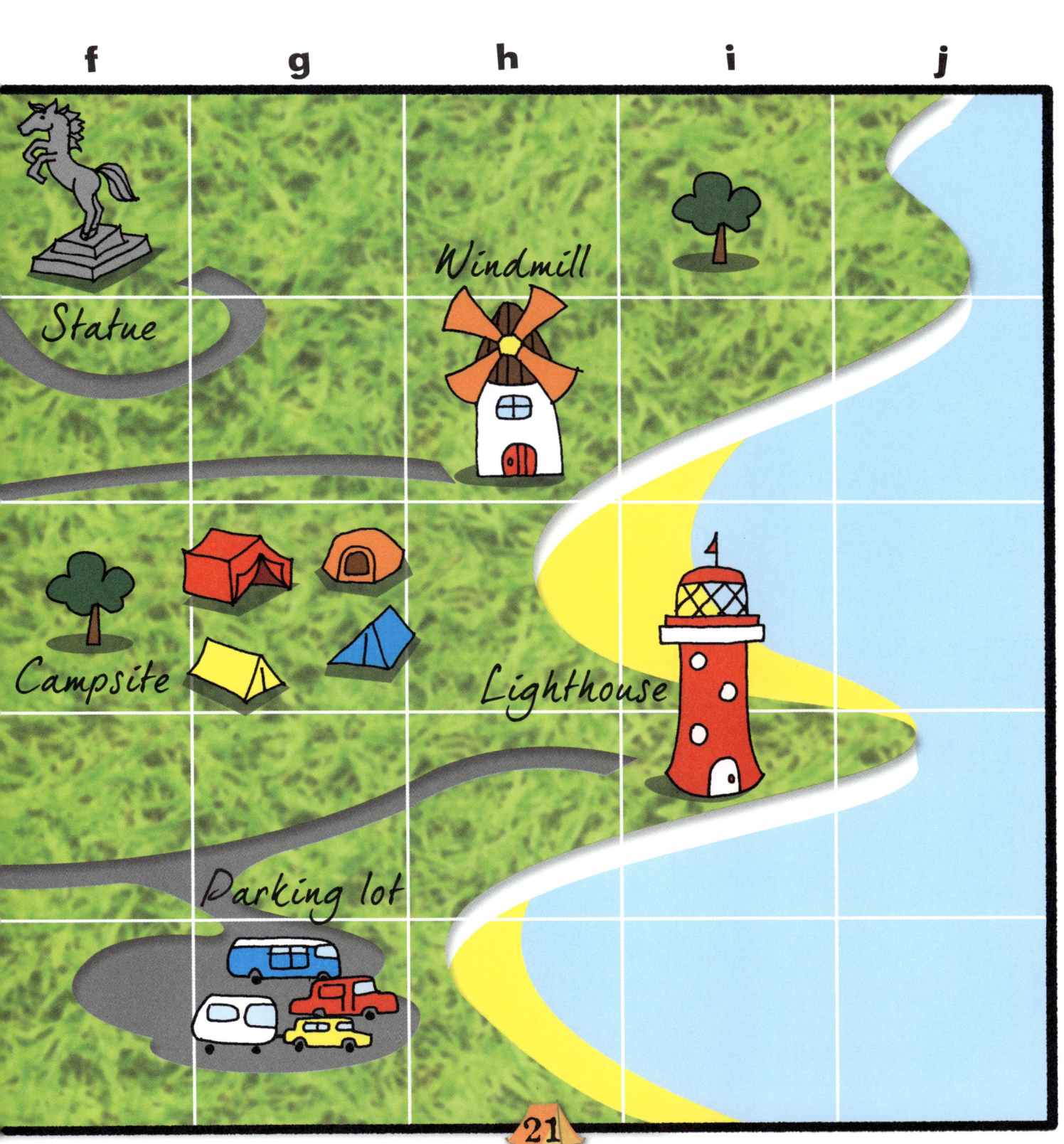

Join in a sing-along with this great musical shaker. It is easy to make and play.

You will need: card stock, cardboard tube, scissors, glue, felt-tip markers, kitchen foil, and dried beans like lentils or split peas.

1 Trace the end of the tube onto two pieces of card stock. Draw a larger circle around each of the traced circles.

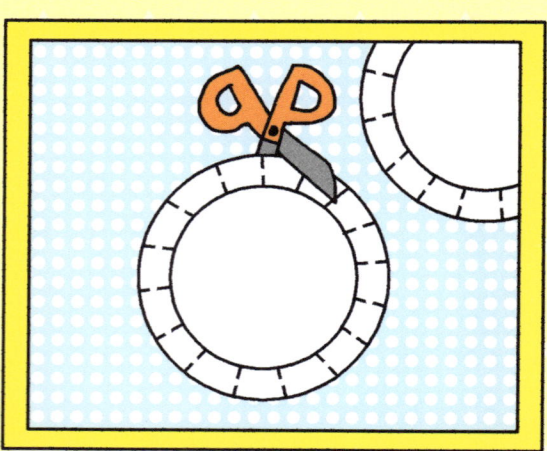

2 Cut out the larger circles. Snip toward the inner circles (as indicated by dashed lines).

22

3 Spread glue onto the snipped sections of one circle.

4 Glue it to seal one end of the tube.

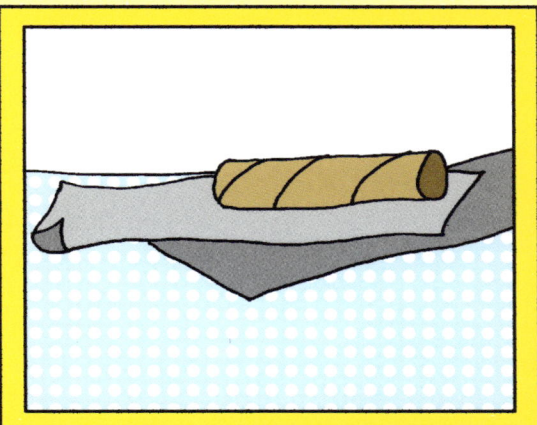

5 Cut two pieces of kitchen foil one and a half times the length of the tube.

6 Scrunch and twist them into coils and place them inside the tube.

7 Pour a cup of dried beans into the tube. Seal the other end of the tube by gluing the remaining disk into place.

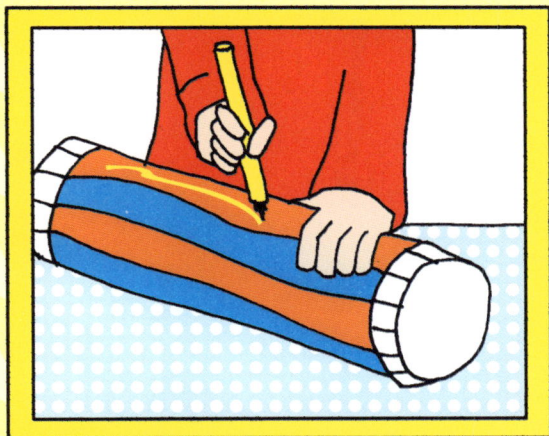

8 Decorate the tube with strips of paper or color it with felt-tip markers.

Can you spot eight differences between these two pictures? Circle them as you find them.

A great way to scare your friends, especially when camping!

You will need: sheets of card stock, scissors, sticky tape, sticks, and a torch.

1 Copy or trace the monster templates (below) onto the card stock. Cut them out.

2 Tape each monster to the top of a stick.

3 When it is dark (or in a darkened room), shine the torch onto the monster so it projects onto a wall. If camping, stand outside the tent and project the silhouette onto the wall of the tent.

4 To make your monster appear to move, start close to the wall (the monster will be small) and then walk away (the silhouette will get larger).

Templates

Using the stickers from the sticker pages, finish the maze then find your way through it.

26

Finish

It's fun to lie on a blanket on a warm starry night and gaze at the stars. Use the star stickers on the sticker pages to make constellations.

29

Make a cool wind chime for your room.

You will need: two sticks about 6 inches long, ball of string, scissors, and a collection of things that can be threaded (buttons, shells, pebbles with holes).

1 Make the crossbar by securely lashing the stickers together with string.

2 Cut pieces of string, about 8 inches long. You will need a piece of string for each item going on your mobile. Twelve to sixteen dangling threads will look good. Tie a large knot in one end of the string, then thread on the button or shell.

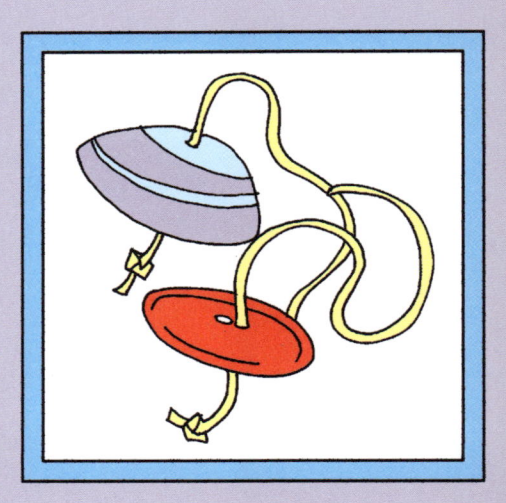

3 Tie the threaded strings to the crossbars so the shells or buttons are level and will clink against each other to make a noise.

4 Tie a loop of string to the crossbars so that you can hang the chimes in your room.

Keep your vacation memories on this page. Tape pictures, tickets, and souvenirs here and don't forget to label them.

Photos

Interesting things

Answers

Page 7
Ellie – yellow sleeping bag
Craig – orange sleeping bag
Amy – red sleeping bag
Tyler – green sleeping bag

Page 10
(crossword)
1. mallet
2. sleeping bag
3. groundsheet
4. tent
4. pegs
5. picnic
6. torch

Page 11
Camper van

Page 14/15

Page 16
(word search)

Page 17
a - owl
b - fox
c - bat
d - mouse
e - deer

Page 19
Carrie – a
Tony – e
Rachel – b
Scott – d
Dean – c

Page 20
b4 – Lake
d5 – Castle
f1 – Statue
g5 – Parking Lot
h2 – Windmill
i4 – Lighthouse

Page 24

Page 26/27

These stickers are just for fun!

These stickers are just for fun!